THE WOUND-DRESSER'S DREAM

Books by Pauline Stainer

Little Egypt (Smith/Doorstop Books, 1987)

The Honeycomb (Bloodaxe Books, 1989)
WITH ILLUSTRATIONS BY BRIAN PARTRIDGE

Sighting the Slave Ship (Bloodaxe Books, 1992)

The Ice-Pilot Speaks (Bloodaxe Books, 1994)

The No-Man's Tree (MakingWaves, 1994)
SELECTED POEMS TRANSLATED FROM THE NORWEGIAN
BY ÅSE-MARIE NESSE AND PAULINE STAINER

Salt over Skara Brae (Prospero Poets, 1995)
WITH ILLUSTRATIONS BY JOSEPH HEWES

The Wound-dresser's Dream (Bloodaxe Books, 1996)

PAULINE STAINER

✦

THE

Wound-dresser's Dream

BLOODAXE BOOKS

ISBN: 1 85224 370 8

First published 1996 by
Bloodaxe Books Ltd,
P.O. Box 1SN,
Newcastle upon Tyne NE99 1SN.

Bloodaxe Books Ltd acknowledges
the financial assistance of Northern Arts.

Cover printing by J. Thomson Colour Printers Ltd, Glasgow.

Printed in Great Britain by
Cromwell Press Ltd, Broughton Gifford, Melksham, Wiltshire.

For D

Acknowledgements

Acknowledgements are due to the editors of the following publications in which some of these poems first appeared: *The Antigonish Review*, *Blue Cage*, *Images*, *The Interpreter's House*, *Lines Review*, *New Welsh Review*, *Odyssey*, *Other Poetry*, *Oxford Magazine*, *Poetry Review*, *Prospice*, *The Rialto*, *Stand*, *Tabla* and *Terrible Work*.

The sequence *Music for Kshantivada* appeared in *New Writing 5*, published by Vintage in association with the British Council. 'Wound for a Crucifixion' (now revised) was commissioned by The Drama House for *Words from Jerusalem* shown on BBC-1. 'White Man Sleeps' was commissioned by the Advice Arcade, Norwich, for the exhibition *Writing on the Wall*.

Other poems draw upon various sources: 'Waterfalls': William Carlos Williams; 'Keats on Iona': Oscar Wilde; 'The Wound-dresser's Dream': John Berryman, Stanley Spencer, Salvador Dalí; 'Lindow Man': John Ruskin; 'Chromatics': Francis Bacon; 'This Accomplishing of Light': Egon Schiele, Giles Foden; 'Wound for a Crucifixion': Giorgio di Chirico, Samuel Beckett, John Damascene; 'The Rubric': Wallace Stevens; 'The Ballerina': Tennessee Williams; 'Buddhas': Jean Genet, James Hamilton-Paterson; 'Music for Kshantivada': Evan Eisenberg, Joseph Conrad.

Contents

Fidra's Song

(for David at Orinsay)

I

I hear a sound in the distance
hares in the open,
hawks digesting bone

an ivory scoop
clearing the breathing-hole
of the seal

oracles incised
with inscriptions
about rain

machines that tunnel
so silently, dice no longer
jump on a drumskin

the little gag of felt,
moonshine and lion
left to bury the dead.

II

The ear is pricked to
the sound of light itself

small flashing cymbals
as the sungod weeps bees

trumpets in the long moon
voces angelicae, flawless, waterworn

when the waves
are short singable lines

and the tongue moves by itself
Donne ch'avete intelletto d'amore

III

What is the look of the sound?

Any pressure on the black mosses
produces a kind of weeping

the moon beats its silk drum,
windows flex in the sea-wind

and the god of rainwater
lets lilies fall from his mouth.

IV

I saw three ships come
to the offshore isle

the lochan sullen with sky,
salt-lamb on the yellow wrack

the dead taking vehicles of enlightenment
over billowed vertebrae

thin strips of sheet-gold
ran down their cheeks

I couldn't bury her on a Sunday
but put a warm stone

into the vanishing cabinet
of the heart

and between fragrant rushes
the necessary beasts

bright with humility
graze the lazybeds.

Gilgamesh

In the mountain pass
he watched the lions play
by moonlight

their manes electric-blue,
the stars percussionists
through the frost.

Raging, he tore them
limb from limb,
ripped out their hearts.

Years later
they rose up before him
in the underworld

shook their manes
like shining turbines
through the updraught

until the fever-blisters
broke out on his lip –
and remembering

the hanging fire
of their wounds,
he felt again

the strange *rubato*
of his own heart
beating with theirs

for several minutes
after extraction.

Darwin in Patagonia

I brood on the process
of perfection and the less
perfectly gliding squirrels

in the parallel light of the afternoons
I study the creatures
constructed for twilight

I am never completely well;
the lakes hang like mica templates
in the brackish air

the winds pour from La Plata,
flies breed in the navels
of young mammals

I record the diving thrushes,
the woodpeckers
in the treeless wastes

the ice floes
which may formerly
have transported foxes;

across the straits
the barbarians multiply
The horse among the trumpets saith 'Aha!'

I take quinine and speculate
on the slashing claw
in the folded schists

but still dream
of Adam naming
the doubtful species

and wake shuddering
at the irreproachable design
of the eye.

The creatures preach to St Francis

They speak through my wounds
whether out of the body I cannot tell

the lion's eardrum flexing to the bees
in its own carcass

otters coupling in the burial boat

the stoat
who dances the questions put to him

reindeer sinews
lowering coffins through the ice

the mongoose tonguing the wind
from the feet of the dead

the muzzle of the snow-leopard
no more than after-image
in the extreme frost.

Magi

They wear sulphur tints.

But when they come close
they do not look like those
who can speak of perfection

for their mouths are iced over
and must be broken open.

The Museum of Childhood glimpsed from the train

I had nothing to love

Ruskin,
unwrapping the Punch and Judy dolls
before his mother confiscates them
(clad in scarlet and gold,
dancing when tied
to the leg of a chair).

I never saw them again

Bergman, filching
his brother's magic lantern
into the wardrobe,
cranking the handle
to the smell of mothballs
and hot metal.

I had never seen any grief

Peep into the portable diorama:
De Quincey,
backlit,
as he stole upon
his dead sister
in a sunlit room.

Ruskin takes Rose La Touche to the Crystal Palace

I

How circumspect they are
under the cast iron,
their figures reduced
as in a *camera lucida*.

They do not touch
although fountains
solicit the humid air
and Amazonian lilies

carry cargoes
of quicksilver
to enhance
her pallor.

But he trembles
at her slight body
solarised against
the glazing-bars,

the sun behind
the quinine tree
swinging
its polished axe.

II

Unable to sleep,
he heard the rail-wagons
laden with gypsum
smoke past.

She had coughed
in the rising dust
as he showed her the casts
of plaster virgins.

And as they left,
those two mutes in the street;
the sound of drilling
in the cold moist air.

III

Above the waterfall
the river is dark
as silveret.

He could have knelt
as she turned
laughing

and thrown bright drops
upon the breasts
he dared not touch.

IV

As a boy on Chamonix
he had measured
the intensity of blue
with a cyanometer.

But what is the killing blue
that makes him kneel
suddenly on Skiddaw
and invoke the Litany,

her letter in his breast-pocket
between gold plates so thin
the snowline burns through them
purple and green?

Waterfalls

are hard to interpret

Hokusai caught them
dropping rods of quartz
into the core of the eye.

But I see them
lean glass easels
against the sun

giving only veiled replies
as the firing squad
pose for the camera.

By an unknown photographer

The lake is quite circular
and linen is left to bleach
under the salt bushes

the air full of unfired pigments –
the lightning man with axes
at elbow and foot

floating islands of peat
giving off a sweet savour
as they burn

but nothing ignites the trance
until the swans come in their thousands
and drink from the solid light

without breaking the seal.

Carol

There's a print on the grass
where she lay, she lay

there's dew on the thorn
where she rapt him away

there's white over green
where she gave him the breast

sancta
sancta simplicitas

O queen of bliss
in the hawthorn shade

O white under white
of the Christchild laid

like a tear, like a tear
in a stem of glass

sancta
sancta simplicitas

Salthouse

Here, angels hold up
the corners of the light
and let it drop

flints flash the sun,
the four beasts smile,
The milde lomb is sprad o rode

while the Queen of Sheba
mistaking the sea of glass
for water

lifts up her robe
before Solomon.

Keats on Iona

Did he hear
the four beasts
saying *Amen*
in the tall rain

did he see
Ezekiel
white-blind a moment
in the magnesium flare

did he taste the salt
on Salomé's neck,
a bubble of blood
rising in his throat

as the pearls
expire on her flesh?

Dancing the Mysteries

'I am the Word who did dance all things.'

Tinctura Sacra

Determined
to speak at the Synod
about sexual love between men,

and knowing death to be
the undisclosed miracle,
you postponed the operation for two weeks.

Three times in five years,
surgeons will expose the brain,
remove the tumour;

diminish sight and speech
with scalpels
of divining-silver.

But love is more
than its own likeness.
In the stern theatre

it is Cordelia
who plays the Fool.

Dancing the Mysteries is an elegy for a priest: Peter Elers of Thaxted,
Essex. The Fourth Thaxted bell is known as 'The Dance Bell' and
bears the inscription 'I ring for the General Dance', taken from an
old Cornish carol, 'The Dancing Day'. Both this carol and the Morris
dancers are traditionally associated with Thaxted.

Recasting the Bell
I ring for The General Dance

At the foundry,
men from the Morris Ring
gather for the casting.

The bell-mould bears
musicians, embossed dancers,
the hand of the Baptist.

They shield their eyes
against bright spillage
into cymbal, string and pipe.

Such emblems from the furnace –
the glowing throat of the bell
in the casting-pit,

the blaze in the clay;
and when the frieze of dancers
sheds its mould,

the rung-changes.

The Master Class

A consort are playing
Easter music at the hospice,
fantasias for viols.

Those who listen
are the benign
with aggressive tumours.

Notes fall like pencil-crystals:
lacrimae Christi
for the sickness unto death.

Is ripeness all,
when the dying are touched
by the inconsolable urgency of the flesh,

the rising thirst
intoned by the priest
on Good Friday?

The musicians bow
spiritual exercises,
suspensions, falling thirds;

silver-point studies
for a crucifixion,
Missa quinta toni.

Harmonics so tender
they might be intravenous,
tilt to the light;

and for a moment
bodies are no more
than counterweights of perspex

and listening blood
a fugue in red.

Dancing the Mysteries

I

*We'll come to the funeral
and how shall we dress?*

The Morris men
in waistcoats and white trousers
kneel at the altar-rail
after the elevation of the Host.

Breath and incense
cloud the chill air.

II

He has chosen his partner
from the dancing-ring;
Sing levy dew, sing levy dew.

The lissom boys
red satin wore
for Corpus Christi Day.

III

Outside the west door,
the Morris men dance
in the graveyard
with flowers in their hats.

But one –
the dancing-partner
playing the Fool,
in scarlet so red –

the white bloom
of his body,
the red stoup
of his blood –

ah dancer, ah sweet dancer

death
is the sun dancing.

Perfect Fifths

He wears
the purple sash of Lent
to the feast;
cannot drink
without slurping.

He, who was eloquent,
can no longer speak
of how the dove
hides
its illumined breast.

It is time for communion:
he cannot swallow
the wine;
is one of the wordless
who take the Word on their tongue.

But he listens
as we switch the tapes
at his bedside –
to the rising perfect fifths
for the raising of Lazarus.

Iron Stella
(for Gill)

Here, where once
we saw the vibration of cellos
rouse bats from the transepts,
there is only the great iron stella
between congregation and coffin.

'The rightness of the ritual,' you said;
a corona
for solder-lines on the skull;
bright salts from the furnace
for the office of the heart.

At the concerto,
spirits had flickered
between the stations of the cross –
the tinge of diastole
swept the white stone.

Strange visitation
in the deepening dusk:
to feel the pulse of music
after pall-weight,
the arteried bone,

the quickening
of the grafted thorn.

White Lent

Street-children
sing their garland
with backs to the dying

O Mary, O Mary
your true love is dead.
The robes they lay in fold.

The fair linen,
salt and candle,
burning-perfume of wounds.

Madonna of the goldfinch,
give us
tapers of chrism –

the lighting of lesions
is the game
in the rose-garden.

A Cherry-Tree Carol

With chalice and paten
by the bare spring tree,
tomorrow shall be my dancing day.

By the tower windmill –
its occasional creak against the sky –
tomorrow shall be my dancing day.

O lily-white boys
at the grave's dark lip
tomorrow shall be my dancing day.

The fantail spins,
the shining sails turn into the wind;
tomorrow shall be my dancing day.

'And having danced these things with us, Beloved, the Lord went forth.
And we, as though beside ourselves, or wakened out of deep sleep, fled
each our several ways.'

A Christening by Snowlight

She had wanted you
christened between waters.

In the bridge-chapel
there was always
the intravenous lilt
of the river
flowing blackly below.

We stood in a light trance,
snow its own ceremony,
underglow of wax-myrtle
from the font
and as the priest tilted
the ewer,
the milk welling
like a hot tincture
inside her blouse.

The Sculpture Museum in February

It was warm behind the glass,
the sun a swung lure

chandeliers filmed with muslin,
marble bodies flowing against the light

so many sexual positions
ghosted in the huge milky mirrors

and outside, the rococo garden,
a gardener opening the soil.

The Ageing of the Snow Crystal

Translation

Below the glacier
the gondolas swing
along the lower slopes.

We lay there once
in vanished shadow
of the stooping buzzard

slept on the fallow field
like the legendary hare
with eyes open

phosphored
breast to breast
upon faint dew

nor heard the owl
in the estranging elder
bodies translated so.

Chill-factor

You are above 10,000 feet
Watch your heart
the aerial cableway
dizzies into the blizzard.

Is it cold so quickly –
ravens circling below
on the thermals,
precipitation

the graffiti of lovers
on the ice pillar?

Bedrock

In the temperate glacier
the top ice flows faster

O we flowed once –
before ice tongued the bedrock
and unequal melting
rippled the stone.

Men carve a grotto
into the summit ice;
they are spattered
with crescent-scars

like those who cut
Carrara marble
with diamond-toothed saws
to sculpt the Madonna.

Nothing is inviolate –
even the heart
chipped from
its summer deposits

piecemeal

Double Portrait (with lover)

They have sited
a maze of mirrors
in the transverse gallery
of the glacier.

We loved by mirrors,
detected by touch
what is real
and unreal

amazed each other
into diagrams of silence
while fresh-fallen hexagons
softened the snow–cornice.

It is witchcraft –
the collusion
under the microscope,
the ageing of the snow crystal

while the heart
holds afterburn.

Through-shine

They say melting and re-freezing
causes colours –
the heart is nothing
if not spectacular

glacier fish
fume-up like metaphor
to the milky bubbles
of ancient atmospheres

here the ice is clouded
with pollen-grains,
the philtred fragrance
of organic dusts

ultra-violet blooms
through their inclusions,
a raven swings
by its feet

undecayed.
What do the snowblind see
when wounds are
no longer red?

Noli me tangere

Who are they,
the snowblind
in the glacier garden
where the meltwater jet
scours the rockflow
and the palmleaf prints
the ammonite?

Will they touch
as they did
when they knew one another,
Christ rolling back
the ripple-stone
between the phases
of alpine folding

to earth
the Magdalen
like sheet-lightning?

Nightingales at Fingringhoe

How downbeat they looked
with their whitish breasts
in the underbrush

the estuary wearing
the moon at its throat,
the Queen Anne's Lace levitating,

a ship of blued-steel
drawn silently seaward
through the salt-marsh

as if it heard, beyond such song,
that other siren
of the young owls calling.

The Inland Boat

It was beached high
on the salt-marsh
under Spanish chestnuts.

We lay on the bleached boards,
samphire flowing
round the prow.

If we moved with the tide
it was simply electrolytes
in the blood

for at dawn, a stag
threshed its antlers
with the low branches

and we saw the sun rise
through the shed velvet,
salt still on our lips.

Samphire Island

When I think of them,
the samphire still
takes me yellowly
by the throat

the lepidopterists –
dragging their generator
down to the shingle
under a full moon

their wax-spirit figures
doubled by shadows,
moths singeing their silks
in the salt dazzle

and high above,
the ripple in the rock,
stone coffins
swilling with rainwater.

The Bone Orchard

In my dream
I saw an orchard of bone,
occasional weapons
still protruding
from the spine

arrested growth-lines
dripping with Spanish moss,
calcified cysts,
silver bullion
under the moon.

So why didn't I wake
hungry for those fevers
that like love
or isolated acts of kindness
leave no mark on the bone?

The Sleep Laboratory

We sleep lightly,
the moon irresolute
behind high fast cloud,
our rapid eye movements
monitored

precision instruments
for dreaming,
our temples wired
as the wild geese
fly over.

But nothing registers
the waking dream –
that glimpse of livid hellebore
in the unploughed square
under the pylon

Persephone
for the flower she once plucked.

White Man Sleeps

(after Barbara Leaney)

O wave and particle –
how shall we earth
this controlled floating,
the fibre optics,
the soft embalming?

Cables sing
of the space around bones,
the crown of hair,
the stiff gold wires
cast down, cast down.

The pyramids soak up dream
like gorgon's blood;
under the lids
the heightened red
is hard and clear as resin

the pupil
a drilled hole;
how shall it tell
the quality of moonlight
on the sleepless?

dreams have no
inessentials
the ancestors lie
with electrodes
at their bluish temples

the fiction
of the body
to compose electronic music
in a city
without power.

After the bread-queue massacre

in Sarajevo,
Vedran Smailović puts on
white tie and tails
and plays Albinoni
among the ruins.

It is May –
blue with the outbreath
of swallows,
the gaze struck away
by the dazzle, the rubble

and at the edge of hearing
the sound for which
there is no music –
the dismembered
re-assembling their limbs.

The Wound-dresser's Dream

In May 1819, John Keats considered signing on as a ship's surgeon.

I

The sirens are those journeys
we never make,
compulsory territories
fabulous as blood,

the dog-star rising
over the cobalt mines,
shafts of flywheels
inflecting the engine-room.

What drums
on the sun's image
is the art
of the unlooked for,

swans dyed russet
by heavy metals,
wax figurines
under the embalming-wound,

that chance cargo
of boat people
in sacrificial dress
for the scenting of icebergs.

II

Do you not hear the sea?

I read *Lear* in the ship's pharmacy.
The crew pray
and clean their weapons,
birds rise like grapeshot
into the Egyptian blue,

the ship ghosting
the Sargasso,
only a mizzen raised
above the ambergris
and floating weed.

We sleep lightly
as falconers,
our cargo of quicksilver
soughing against
the sun,

no dew, no dew,
only incidental bleeding.
On the 6th.
the large white pig
executed on a curved ocean,

the baffled air
full of wild ginger,
the masts dropping
medicinal gums
into the sirocco.

Such investiture
of salt
I cough my proper blood
and digest nothing
but milk.

III

In the sail-maker's loft
we watched the great moon-moths
mate on the folded sails

compound insatiate ghosts
secreting syrups
against the glisten of salt.

Above, the shrouds belling,
and ashore, the sound of
heavy firing in the hills,

the wounded with their faces
covered in little squares
of mosquito-netting

IV

We anchor off the ice-plinth.
Is there no language
to localise pain?

We bleed the source,
sense the frazil-ice
through the hull

the scream of the ermine
frozen by its tongue
to the trapper's salt-lick

the sacred conversation
of sleighs shod with runners
of jawbone

the bluish foxes
that search
through a mountain of shoes

the silver-backed jackals.

V

In the room
off the Spanish steps
the tiny rattle
of salt through sea-lavender,
the sound of nuns
in habits blue as chicory
singing the sevenfold *Amen.*

Sweetwater rises
through the shingle,
the land-wind
green with pollen,
Xenophon's men still lying
honeyed
under the toxic rhododendron.

Heavy artillery
moves into the marsh samphires.
Without morphine
the medical orderly
at the battle of Grodek
cannot fit the look of wounds
into any imaginable world.

The white clinic falls silent
round the pure chromolithography
of a lung

In the wound-dresser's dream
the eyes of the beloved
are washed with milk.

Cutting the Hare

What would the Green Children
have made of it –

the standing blood of the hare
in the standing corn

reapers advancing on
the last uncut square?

And coming from twilight
as they did

what language
could they possibly have had

when he broke cover,
men and dogs in pursuit,

for his red tangent
across the green retina?

Lindow Man

No words that I know of
will say what mosses are
yet we disturbed you
in the ancient sphagnum,
found mistletoe in your gut.

So what is unspeakable?
The sacred wound,
the triple death,
or simply sunlight
repeating such fiction?

The Wind Farm

perpetuum mobile
fifteen windmills
in a rippling landscape

the white whoosh
of their arms tilting
at corn circles

Don Quixote
reeling from the
Body Electric.

Swallows at the Alhambra
(for Gareth)

How can the light allow
so many soloists,
hot-blooded, contrapuntal

fantasia upon one note
as the lotus pool
barely overflows?

Coleridge goes scuba-diving

How it intoxicates –
to have air for half an hour

the sea-bed
a quilt of India stuff
tasselled and fringed

a pillar of krill
passing through me
in *corpo transparente*

the flashing cipher
of eels as they graze
my wetsuit

glass-fish
with invisible viscera,
floaters in an eye

and even here
that other implausible cargo –
afterimage –

the swallow
supporting the sun
on one wing.

Chromatics

(after Marianne Kirchgessner)

I am the touch player –
the blind girl
at the glass harmonica,
running wet fingers
round the rim
of each revolving bowl.

I perform for Mozart
in his satin frockcoat;
they tell me his scores are immaculate,
that the division
has an agreement
with the glittering of light.

When I work the treadle
I feel the altered element –
fiery circles,
the susceptibility of things
to hold colours
not their own.

But how does the ear
conjure the eye
when, playing to an audience,
I hear the glass-blower's breath
flood each of their heart-chambers
in turn?

This Accomplishing of Light

(Florence, 1994)

I

You stood at the open window
dark with your own brilliance

and I, watching the light
touch nipple and lip
through the blown curtain

could think of nothing
but St Francis preaching
to the waterfall

and the running line of your breasts
between two waters.

II

I paint the light
that comes out of the body
as the glass flexes
and the Madonna conceives
through a slit
at the stomach
of her unbuttoned dress.

III

He has manifested himself
through the body

the burn of the moment
an iodide of silver

absolutely unalterable
in sunlight.

IV

What was in these bodies
that was so distinctly known?

Baroque violins
have a thread of metal
pressed into the gut.

Light whirrs;
the wind lifts gold leaf
with a squirrel's tail

the glitter on the string
like music.

V

It is noon; the bridge
rising over the river on mortar
made from egg-whites;

the lovers dovetail,
light passing through them
unabsorbed;

nor do they move
through time or space
any more than those magnets

hung in great telescopes
from spider's silk
that never twists.

VI

She stooping,
he with his head
against her belly,
the linen
wrapped round her thighs
like a mummy.

Which flows –
light or the body,
when the mirror
milks her skin,
and the sun through her lids
externalises the blood?

The anonymous Italian master
seeks the lightest tone
matizatura
for those signs
made on the body
and carried in the heart:

the disciple
with traces of gilding;
the angel isolate
against silk panels;
blood-sugars
of the golden bird.

VII *Fragment after Piero della Francesca*

Light fails

but not the process
of shining,

those wilder
less mimetic shores

where the dove
releases itself

from its white horizontal.

Pietà

I

I am the lady
with the fool in my lap.
Anatomise him then.

You will see
from his physiology
that spirits are accurate beings;

the pain-threshold
determined by deviation,
tilted navel, halo off-centre,

ankle and elbow
angled like star-maps
against the grid.

Who would expect
the racked body
to have perfect proportions –

the exactitude of dying
to be rising diagonals
on the heart's field –

the socket of the eye
to belie
the sorcery of the circle's edge?

II

And my poor fool is hanged
pigments of white-lead
highlight his flesh;

bloodstone
and leopard's tooth
burnish his brow.

Here is watered ink
from the squirrel-brush,
willow-charcoal for sketching;

earth-green and cinnabar
layered along the axis
of the axle-tree.

III

I would limn him without shadow;
bleach the blood alleys;
paint-out his wounds.

Hang him again
on gessoed ground
weightless as a wren-king.

Align him
on the passionate template,
cross-stitch his shroud.

Pity asks perfect tension –
the body slackening
after deposition –

particularity
as revelation.

Wound for a Crucifixion

(after Francis Bacon)

I

It could be any wound
undulating down the cross

art's otherness, like calvary,
an accidental in the flesh

but what was the look of the wound
before his looking altered it?

II

At the foot of the cross, Mary Magdalen
gathers all reds into her robe.

Wherever she moves
the wounds move with her

and burn through her tears,
incisions in a balsam tree.

The little foxes from the vineyards
look out through his side.

What is the gist of suffering
when the fountain plays with its own loss?

III

Put your ear to the shiver-tree.
Hear the throb of the wound

pulsar obligato, pitted against live players,
percussion scoring for skins and metal only

five distances for five instruments
vasts apart

How shall we pitch it right
when what engineers the blood

is still the dream
accompanied by a sense of touch

the angel coming quickly
while rodents notch the longbones?

IV

At the moment of truth
there are no understudies in the pit

Christ hangs between terrorists;
immortality ticks

the body wired to dynamite
shalt be with me in Paradise

V

Our Lady of the Rose-trellis
where the Christ-child plays the zither

Our Lady of the Pasture
sown with butterfly mines

Our Lady of the Saltings
where eels, drawn by hot effluents

eat out the fresh red heartwood –
do not weep at his *wonderful condescension*

the dogwoods redden
there's a lull in the killing

and with the lassitude of the infinite
Christ's wounds re-align their diagonals.

The Exchange

It was Ash Wednesday

the church green sandstone,
angels with crossed ankles
in the amber glass,

a crusader knight
resting spurs
on the lion at his feet,

his lady still in childbed
against the louring light.
Such sleeping red

we laid hands
rank with wild garlic
on her slashed sleeves

and like lovers exchanging bodies
shivered a moment,
burned.

The Etching

I drew your body
directly on the plate,
slid the zinc
into warm acid –
brushed the bubbles
from the slight swell of your belly
with a feather.

Solvent and ghost –
as when we made love
like silkmoths
dissolving their own shroud,
outside, the men
laying cat's eyes,
and we unselved.

The Feather

(after Calvino)

And when Jesus came
to the ruler's house
and saw the flute players
he said 'Depart,
for the girl is not dead
but sleeping'.

Did he know
when he went in
and took her by the hand
that the hieroglyph
for the weighing of souls
was also the fundamental note
of the flute?

The Burgomaster's Daughter

(Leipzig, 1945)

Why do they wait
the soldiers at the door,
she on the black-buttoned
sofa alone?

The light falls on her lapels
like drinkable gold,
the fillings in her teeth
red-gold as her hair.

Why don't they flinch
the allies at the door?
O make my bed father
for I fain would lie down.

The Rubric

Efficiency is humane
written in red
on the rising dust
from the bone-milling machine.

I heard
the cry of its occasion
as the Carmelite sisters
at Auschwitz

sang a little requiem
for Primo Levi
and took the scarlet wafer
on their tongues.

The Ballerina
(after Frida Kahlo)

The surgeon runs a hand
down her bone-grafts.

She will paint the spine
cracked into oracle,
each rivet its own shadow.

In Mexico City
the bus-crash threw gold-dust
over her body.

Seeing the spangle in her blood
the passengers cried
'la bailarina, la bailarina'.

Her breasts blossom
through the surgical corset
flores, flores por los muertos!

Unearthing dancers along the Silk Road

I will lay sinews upon you
in your white clay slip

until the breeze fills
your terracotta sleeves

and leaving the mulberry orchards
you reach the red shales

where the shadows of isolated trees
stretch great distances

and giddy for the presence of water
you come upon

rock-roses, exuding resin
like vast dew.

Variations on a black-chalk drawing of Jesuit missionaries in Chinese dress

I

It is the Octave of Innocents;
snow falls
on the Silk Road

and the odd bird flies past
like one of those angels
below the level of the crucified.

II

It has rained;
warm mists run up
from the cinnabar mines,
the river yellow
with the upturned bellies
of rats flushed from the granary.

Downstream, cormorant fishers
blow the coals
on their floating clay hearths.

The priests pause a moment
on the cable-bridge,
drawn to the lit discipline
of birds, diving with hooped gullets
from a glistening leash.

And beyond, between the angelica,
the city surprises the shifting marsh
with occasional fireworks at night.

III

Since Ash Wednesday
they have worn their penitence
like salt-glaze.

No need to mortify the flesh –
the wind has jade
sewn into its robe

and sturgeon hurl themselves
at the overfall
in the melting hail.

After siting the spirit road

horse and rider
all gaze the same way
in the rising rice-fields

and tomb felines,
too incurious to read
the running of the winged deer

cause a slow echo
as circular jades
fall from their eyes.

Gesualdo

He rocks his baby to death
dumb like the lamb
before its shearer

It is Holy Week;
the responses for Tenebrae
lie on the cassone.

Which gives the swifter blood-sugar –
setting the Five Wounds
for boys' voices

or the scream
of the mating vixen
as he swings the cradle faster?

The Geometrical Ascent to the Gallery

Every day at dawn
he installed himself
in the Bull's Eye chamber
of the cathedral lantern,
sketched the panorama
in the pure air, before fires were lit.

He carried up graphic telescopes,
constructed an observatory
above the cross and ball,
a cabin on castors
rotating
through whispering hawsers.

Coming down from the scaffold,
the river a watered-steel blade,
he would press himself
to the external ladders
dizzied, not knowing
if the slight vibration

was an antiphon
of boys' voices
rising inside the dome,
or simply Christ
breaking his buffeted body
before the disciples.

Freefall

I am expert
at deferring the death-wish.

If I look down
it is through the eye
of a beading-needle,
fallows pencilled in
under the passage hawks,
fairground roundabouts
like coloured cogs.

Delay elates –
I plunge without
a bloom on the lens,
the air a glass-blank
complex as silk –
survival
that fatal instinct

which lets rip the blood.

Buddhas

do not even
have the grace
of seeming perishable.

What do they make
of the *whizzing imperative*

when autumn bleeds at the edges

and the starving
eat lilies and wild honey?

Dance with a metal coat

The stage is steel –
rusted, beaten, burnished
by Japanese dancers.

They hurl themselves
to no rhythm
but their breathing

and the crackle
as their coats ignite
like water in sunlight.

The moment is melted down –
river and ore,
wave and particle

the gliding sequences
of the body
remaking itself

Seven thunders utter

and in the flash flood
ancestral carp
are flushed from the moat
of the imperial palace

pedestrians struggling up
from the subway
see them stream by
as if from a metal-foil machine

over the zebra crossing
through the traffic lights
past security camera
and the peril of mirrors

until far out
in the suburbs
where the afternoon light
is parallel to the sea

those taking
a remarkable view of bridges
hang over the cutwaters
and glimpse their gilded fins

still snagged
with the blue mosquito nets
and floating sleeves
of the concubines.

Kodo

The great drum sounds
the foetal heartbeat
as the Japanese archer
at full gallop
turns on a hinge of blood
abreast of his quarry
and the Leaping-tiger Garden
does not blink.

Music for Kshantivada

I *Joseph Knecht Tunes the Clavichord*

It is the pure octave he is after –
he lowers his heartrate
like a marksman,
tunes the beating fourths and fifths
to his own pulse.

As master
of the glass bead game
he sets an equal temperament,
no longer hears
how *hazard has such accuracies.*

Suddenly
a billow of scent
through the open window,
soft-focus uprising
of elder in full flower

his heart outpacing
the fourths and fifths,
their impure intervals
flooding him
like an intoxicant

as if the property
of music
were not perfect tuning
but a disparity
that defines.

II *Glossolalia*

In the Japanese temple
the sprung floor
sings when anyone
steps on it

funeral jades
speak through
the nine orifices
of the body

and outside,
the nightingale
rinses the bubble
in its throat.

III *Music for Kshantivada*
(who was dismembered but did not lose his patience)

What engineers the blood
when a severed head sings
of a full moon in March
and the scattered body
remembers music by heart?

Immortality
is the verve of
all that is made,
Isis reassembling
the limbs of Osiris

the high tessitura
with which, in the guise
of a hawk,
she flutters
against the phallus.

IV *Canzone for Tadzio*
(after Britten)

It is the measure of desire
that your body completes the music
before I write even a note

the fish scoring the sea
with their own cross-rhythms
as you dance on the sand

the air ribboned like rococo silk,
the horizon a rim
of running bronze.

So many girdles of gravity –
the wide vibrato
between rods of rolled glass

when you walk
the seven bright gold wires
into the sea.

V *Varèse Improvises the Levitation of the Pyramids*

I require
the most coaxing acoustic –
the quartet
in one movement,
the zither with waxed silk strings.

I introduce
a siren, Chinese blocks,
hawkbells and ocarina,
ghost drum-set,
the roar of the desert lion.

They levitate
to tape alone,
rising *gradazione*
through the haze
by grace of electronics

and as they dream
at altitude,
flexing their photons
against the hot mouth
of the swallow

I build the echo